Dr. Camelia Straughn

Copyright © 2015 Camelia Straughn

All rights reserved. No part of this publication may be reproduced, distributed, or transmitted in any form or by any means, without prior written permission.

Camelia Straughn / RisingSTAR Publishing
Sacramento, California 95822
www.risingstarlifecoach.com

Publisher's Note: This is a work of fiction. Names, characters, places, and incidents are a product of the author's imagination. Locales and public names are sometimes used for atmospheric purposes. Any resemblance to actual people, living or dead, or to businesses, companies, events, institutions, or locales is completely coincidental.

Book Layout © 2014 BookDesignTemplates.com

Finding Your BLISS in the Midst of Pain: 9 Keys to Trusting Yourself and Living an Extraordinary Life / Camelia Straughn -- 1st Ed.
ISBN 978-0-9973607-1-4

Finding Your BLISS in the Midst of Pain

This book is dedicated to all the women who are ready to live their BLISS.

Dr. Camelia Straughn

Contents

INTRODUCTION..7

CHAPTER 1: SEVEN AREAS OF PAIN..............................14

CHAPTER 2: SELF-LOVE TO LOVE...................................29

CHAPTER 3: INTIMACY – IN 2 ME I SEE........................46

CHAPTER 4: FAITH..62

CHAPTER 5: FORGIVENESS..70

CHAPTER 6: SELF-CARE...85

CHAPTER 7: EMPOWERMENT...96

CHAPTER 8: EMBRACING YOU......................................107

CHAPTER 9: FASTING..120

CHAPTER 10: GRATITUDE...129

CHAPTER 11: JOURNAL...137

Finding Your BLISS in the Midst of Pain

A personal Hello for the Author

Peace and blessings, Beautiful Ones. You have the power to create your life to be what you want it to be. So ask yourself, what do you want this life journey to be? Life is wonderful, beautiful even. It is a continuously unfolding story, a story that is unique to you. Everyone's journey is different and that is the beauty to it all.

I have the most amazing time coaching an array of amazing and courageous beings who are ready to share their stories. These amazing beings have embraced the realization that support is most critical as they move through their life cycles.

Many of you are where you are based upon what you believe. We do not ever get what we want; we get what we believe we should have. Do you believe that you are worthy of happiness? Do you believe that happiness, success, abundance, comfort, fulfilment, peace, joy, and love are parts of your birthright? Is this what you believe

Dr. Camelia Straughn

or do you believe something else? You will manifest the life that you believe. Your beliefs are creations, and the sum of all your creations is your life.

Loving you with all the Love in my Heart,

Dr. Camelia Straughn

Finding Your BLISS in the Midst of Pain

Dr. Camelia Straughn

INTRODUCTION

There is something important to remember as you move through this life and that is for every action there is an equal and opposite reaction, what goes out is coming back always, what goes up comes down always. So, in knowing and understanding that know that you are creating everything in your life. There is nothing in this life that is happening out of order. You are creating your life with every thought, every intention, every word and every action. You are co-creating with all the energy of the universe and the more you are aware of that in the most authentic and deepest way the more the energy of the universe rises up to increase your creativity. You and I are co-creating our environment, our friendships, our career, and our love relationships, simply put we are creating us. Stay in the space of that expansive true you and you can never be stuck. Co-creation is the calling of the universe and it is your calling, so get still, expand that awareness of your deepest self and know that your life comes from the same creative force that has created every living thing.

When you are posed with the question "What did you do today?" how do you respond? Most people will respond with talking about the things that happened externally, events from work, school or family life, yet when viewed from the inside out what we're actually doing is very different, everyday each of us is building a self, fulfilling our needs and discovering Who We Are. These inner Activities call for the highest creativity, whatever your level of awareness inner events are happening throughout life and you emerge every day with a changed self, new needs and either grader or lesser self-awareness. All of that is inevitable but you can choose to magnify and accelerate the process or on the other hand to resist and slow it down.

Reality isn't simply out there making demands on you, you are the co-creator of every situation in life and your personal reality is determined by how aware you are of being a co-creator. External situations provide the raw materials only like an artist face with a lump of clay, a blank page or a pallet of colors. You must shape the raw material presented to you if you don't either someone else will or random chance will take over. As your awareness expands your inner contribution will increase an inner contribution can be defined as coming from your true self, the part of you that feels connected to truth,

Finding Your BLISS in the Midst of Pain

beauty, love and evolution. This self wants life to be more purposeful, to have more meaning by comparison if you devote your attention to getting more external rewards they may bring pleasure but rarely bring meaning. A bigger car, more money, a nicer house and so on are not revolutionary when viewed from the inside, from the perspective of your true self.

Building a self that matches your true self is the most creative way to live, when you share your desire to evolve with someone else you form a bond at the level of spirit. Relationships have many purposes yet if you find a partner to travel the path of spiritual unfoldment with you become the ideal co-creator, both of you evolve to a higher personal reality. Co-creating begins with mutual love and support. Sympathizing with each other challenges, fulfilling each other's needs and keeping a higher Vision in sight. You can have the highest kind of created life together, yet the process must begin by relating to yourself with the same love and respect. Consider understanding and accepting the concept "I participate to the fullest in creating my personal reality" (Depak Chopra).

As you move through this book, I want you to ask yourself the question "how bad do you want change". You know the elders used to say "we usually don't make change until we get tired of being tired". Do you have to be tired of being tired before you make a change or do you have the ability that when you recognize that there needs to be change, you make change? It has been proven that it takes approximately 21 to 30 days to change a habit or create a new one, so what I challenge you with is to look inside you, because we all know that you can't change anyone else you can't control anyone else all you can do is change and control you and make change. Look within you or even look outside of you at certain things that are going on that you don't really like or that you know shouldn't be you a part of your life, I would suggest that you look at how you're contributing to that and not only contributing to but also how are you attracting that thing too you.

Then, ask yourself if you really want change. If you do want change then start taking the necessary steps to make that change. Do you really want change, have you actually gotten tired of being tired? Think about that question and ask yourself do you really want to change, do you really want your life to be different, if you do, are you really willing to do what actually needs to be done in order for that to happen? So in looking at that if you really want to change, and you really want things to be different then I would suggest that you look at the situation whatever it may be and do the research, what habits do you need change, what behaviors do you need to adjust, do you need to adjust the circles that you are in and re-evaluate the people type that you're hanging out with. I know that was a lot and it is a lot to think about. But, the reality is you are on your way because you are reading this book. You will find at the end of each chapter I have left some pages blank that are titled notes, this is where you will write your thoughts, lessons learned and reflections. So, breathe, relax and take this journey with me.

CHAPTER 1

SEVEN AREAS OF PAIN

Dr. Camelia Straughn

Check this, Beloved. We all have wounds, we all have experienced hurts, and they come with the territory of living this thing called life. The major issue is not whether or not we are wounded, but rather which of our pains most need our attention. Think now, how are you affected by your wounds? Are you on the path of healing? How can your wounds or pain make you a stronger person, and not just stronger, but better? How can the Creator use you and your wounds for good? In this chapter, we will discuss the seven areas of pain that we may experience. They are emotional, sexual, choices, verbal, social, spiritual, and physical.

Physical Wounds Physical pain is connected to the body and is going to be felt and seen via the body itself. Physical pain can and will range from dis-ease in the body such as disfigurement, confusions, and physical impairment. Physical pain can be a continual reminder that something is wrong. It can show itself in our weight, whether under or over.

We are discussing physical pain and wounds first simply because the world as a whole is obsessed with outer appearance. These wounds are the most visible ones. Think on how you are affected by the physical pain and wounds that you face on a daily basis. Physical wounds are painful by themselves, yet that pain is compounded because it is combined with one or more of the following wounds.

Sexual Wounds Sex is one of the most intimate acts you can participate in with another person. It is also when we are most vulnerable, both physically and spiritually. When another person violates this sacredness, it can leave a gaping hole in our heart, mind, and soul. This pain will run deep and become the reference point of how we see ourselves, others, and life in general. The sexual boundaries that we set serve as a form of protection for us. When those boundaries are violated or crossed - regardless if by force, manipulation, or due to fear - it can, and most times will, render us shattered.

Choice Wounds Sometimes we wallow and linger in our pain when we come to the conclusion that it is due to a choice we made. Sometimes we make nasty, poorly considered, selfish, and foolish choices that create and leave painful scars. We become obsessed with wanting to go back in time, so that we can make a different choice. But here we sit in our thoughts of brokenness with no one to blame but ourselves, which only makes the pain worse.

Verbal Wounds Words can be as painful and as damaging as any physical wound and sometimes even more. So when words of belittlement and demoralization are hurled intentionally or unintentionally by those we love, trust or lean on, and respect, the hurt can pierce us to the very core of our soul. Words of dejection, rejection, or ridicule can easily tear us down, stripping us of our confidence and dreams.

Social Wounds We all want to be liked. So when we feel marginalized, excluded, embarrassed, ignored, used, or attacked by others, the wound is real. Most often, we tell ourselves we are being immature or oversensitive, and we shouldn't hurt. We believe we should be able to ignore our wounds. But this really does nothing to remove the pain. It is important to accept that how people treat us affects us - often profoundly - whether we wish to admit it or not.

Spiritual Wounds Whether we experience hurt by way of the church, synagogue, masjid, religious group or a fellow believer, the clergy or the Creator, the wound can lead to an incisive spiritual loneliness and depression. We feel that if the Creator or his or her people would wound us, He/She must be against us, and does not care about us. Who can stand against the Creator? At this point, our wounds feel like a curse, with no solution and no hope of healing.

Emotional Wounds Each of the above wounds carries with it an emotional component. Sometimes the original wound is buried so deeply in our feelings that we cannot even find it. All we are aware of is a deep, overpowering ache and the emotions that come with it. These strong emotions cloud our judgment, confuse our thinking, and too frequently block awareness that the Creator is beside us.

Here's the thing: our spirit allows us to soar, but our wounds chain us to the ground. Wounds hold us back and force us to lean on the one who can truly heal all wounds. Simply put, there are certain things that do happen and will happen in this life to be the cause of moving us closer to spirit.

So now, what I want you to ask yourself: how is your pain affecting you? It is important not to be afraid to take this journey. I want you to take a moment and read through each symptom below and mark those that you have experienced more than once in the past week. I want you to consider what might be behind each affirmative response. How troublesome are they to the movement of your daily life? As with all the chapters that you will be working through, honesty is going to be your best friend and your greatest ally.

Below you will see a quiz that I researched. Now see where you fit in this. The key at the end of this quiz will help you to see what you need to do next. So, let's put on our big girl or big boy pants and do some inner work. Remember this is all you, you decide and that is a good thing.

- You spontaneously become tearful for no apparent reason.
- You find yourself eating when you're not hungry.
- You are fearful about taking risk.
- It is difficult to truly trust people even yourself.
- At times you do not like yourself.
- Feelings of guilt and shame can be

overwhelming.
- You struggle with periods of deep anger or depression.
- The world doesn't feel like a safe place.
- You wish you could live your life over again.
- You feel like something is wrong with you.
- You are easily frightened.
- You feel lonely and detached from others.
- You do certain things to try to detach yourself from the inner pain.
- Your future doesn't seem very positive.
- It's hard to let go of the past.
- You always expecting something bad to happen.
- Life doesn't seem very fair.
- Nightmares flashbacks or emotional flooding can leave you upset for days.
- Feeling safe and protected is very important to

you.

- It's hard for you to fully relax.

If you checked:

1 - 6   Your wounds are probably mild to moderate - be careful.

7 - 12   Your wounds are probably serious - you need to do something.

13 - 20   Your wounds are probably severe - I would suggest that you look into getting some concentrated help.

Remember this is a tool and your reaction to the information is totally up to you.

The first thing is going to be to not allow this quiz and its results to overwhelm you. Wounds are a part of reality, and reality often offers large doses of hurt and harshness. This does not mean that is what

Finding Your BLISS in the Midst of Pain

your reality has to always be; you are just working at what this moment presents. You have to remember all the good things in your life, and you are one of them.

Another thing we must work to remember - courtesy of Oprah - is that there are no mistakes, there really aren't any, because you have a supreme destiny. When you are in a state of smallness mentally, when you are in your little personality, when you are not centered, you really do not know who you are. You forget that you came from something greater, something bigger, and we all are really the same. When you do not know that, you get irritated and overstressed all the time, wanting something to be what it is not.

Know that there is a supreme moment of destiny calling on your life. Your job is to feel it, to hear it, and to know it. Sometimes, when you are not listening, busy paying bills, or living someone else's dream, you get taken off track. You get into the wrong marriage, the wrong relationship and take the wrong job, but know that it is all leading to the same path. There are no wrong paths, they are just different. There is no such thing as failure, really. That thing or event that you perceive as failure is just that thing trying to move you in another direction.

So you get as much from your losses as you get from your victories. The losses are there to wake you up. The losses remind you of the skills and tools that you need to acquire so that you can get that dream call. When you understand that, you do not allow yourself to be completely thrown by a grade, or about a circumstance. Because your life is bigger than that. Bigger than any experience. Bigger than any circumstance.

So relax, it's going to be okay. Again, relax.

Finding Your BLISS in the Midst of Pain

When you are not at ease with yourself and you're feeling distressed or agitated, that is the universe telling you that you need to be moving in another direction. Do not allow yourself to get completely blown off track and then continue to stay off track.

When you're feeling that you are disoriented that is the key to asking yourself, "How do I turn it around?" The way to get through the challenge is to get still and ask yourself what is the next right move, and the right next move after that, and from that space the next right move after that. Do not get exasperated or start focusing on the circumstance and do not allow yourself to get overwhelmed, because you know your life is bigger than that one moment. You know you are not defined by what someone else says is a failure for you because failure is just that thing that directs you in the right direction.

Dr. Camelia Straughn

NOTES

NOTES

CHAPTER 2 – Key 1

SELF-LOVE TO LOVE

Finding Your BLISS in the Midst of Pain

So you say that you are ready to Love and that you are ready to be loved and you do not understand why they both seem to elude you. Beautiful, I would ask you what your relationship with yourself is. When do you love you? I mean really love you. What do you think about when you are left alone with you? What do you say to yourself or about yourself? Do you still hold on to the relationships and the negative things said in that relationship that did not work?

Beautiful, it is important to recognize that with growth comes change. Sometimes that change comes in the form of a person not being a part of your life anymore. In this chapter, we will discuss the concept of love and we will look at what steps you can take to not only love yourself more but also bring or attract love into your life.

It is our belief that every relationship is only an

arrow towards the ultimate relationship; it is a milestone, it is not a goal. Every love affair is just an indication of a bigger love affair ahead. It is just a little taste, but is that little taste going to quench your thirst or satisfy your hunger? On the contrary, that little taste will make you thirstier, will make you hungrier. That's what happens in most relationships. Rather than giving you contentment, it gives you a tremendous discontent.

Each relationship fails in this world and it is a good thing; it would have been a curse if it was not so. Believe it or not, it is a blessing that it fails. I know it sounds crazy, the truth is that we have to fail a few times to get it right and learn what we need and want. Do not be afraid to end or let go of a relationship that is not fulfilling for you or your partner.

So what is the concept of this thing we call

love? In our research, we find that love is a concept that is bio-social-psychological: genuine love in its non-erotic form typically has a basis in attachment and a social-psychological basis in atonement (shared awareness and identity). Romantic love involves a second physical basis: sexual attraction. Each of these forms can involve very intense feelings. Now all this sounds good and may have a twist of mystery and excitement to it. We all want that love that will create intense feelings within us. After all, if it does not, then it cannot possibly be love.

Beautiful One, it is important to really examine what you envision love to be. What love looks like for you is very different from what it looks like for me, and guess what? That is okay. Believe it or not, the same concept that is used to bring about success can bring forth your perfect love (meaning that perfect love for you, not to be misconstrued as perfect as in no flaws).

But the concept I want you to be clear on first is that of self-love because you will attract what you subconsciously believe you deserve. Before we discuss how to attract love from another into your life, I want you to have a clear understanding of the concept of self-love.

Self-love is the desire or drive to promote one's own well-being. It is an admiration for, or love of, oneself. I know you may be thinking that this makes you selfish. Let's be clear, self-love is not about being inconsiderate of others. It does not mean that you are no longer loving, sympathetic, or understanding to the needs of others. What it does mean is that you treat yourself with kindness, compassion, and understanding just as you would anyone else. When we love ourselves, it creates a guide for others on how to treat us.

Finding Your BLISS in the Midst of Pain

I want you to take a moment and think about what self-love looks like to you. Now that you have a picture based on your idea of self-love, ask are you showing yourself love. Self-love can be: slowing down, letting go, escaping blame, or meditating. Self-love could be as simple as taking a break from self-judgment. For me, when I stop to show self-love, I literally feel like I am taking sandbags off my shoulders which I was not even aware that I was carrying. Things become lighter and I feel free. Now, this lightness can be like an escape from judgment, from feeling unworthy, guilty, or behind the game in some way. It can also look or feel like escaping the pressure of work or it may feel like indulgence. See, self-love can take on many looks and feelings. Simply put, what everyone defines as "being good to yourself" is self-love.

You may be wondering why self-love is so

important. Well, to recap, it will set the standards of how you are treated by others. Now that we have created a clear picture of self-love with an understanding of its importance, we can look at how to attract love into our lives. As you work your way through this chapter, I want you to really stop and think about what you really think that you believe the type of person your mate should be. I want you to consider what you really think and feel about self-love and what you believe you deserve. It is extremely important that you are honest with yourself. Healing cannot come about by sugar-coating what is deep inside of us, even if we deem it as being ugly.

Now, with all of that being said, if you find that you are constantly in relationships that are not healthy for whatever reason, it is time for change. I want you to ask yourself if *you are* ready for a shift,

Finding Your BLISS in the Midst of Pain

are you ready for a change? This shift is going to have to take place both in your subconscious and conscious mind.

To make the shift and make it a lasting one, you must first do some serious *self-evaluation*. I will share some steps and techniques I have learned and used. You can apply these techniques in your life to move forward change, attract, and keep the love you are wanting and needing in your life on a spiritual and physical level. But first I want you to remember and understand that in order to bring forth what you want, you have to believe that you deserve. This is going to be of great importance.

Creating the ideal environment to attract love in one's life

In my research, I have found that there are four core principles to help you release your hidden obstacles to love and become magnetic to your soul mate.

Shifting Your Consciousness This wonderful journey begins with being open to having a shift in consciousness, seeing and clearly accepting how you are the source of your experiences in love. The reality is that everything happens through us, manifesting that thing you have been subconsciously thinking about, be it good or bad. This is a matter of taking personal responsibility. Stop focusing on what the other person did wrong, let go of being a victim. Blame and shame stunts growth. Check your patterns of behaviors. Remember, you can only change you. Our beliefs are the lens through which we are interpreting and then responding to life. Check your thoughts and behaviors and see how you are the source of these patterns. Identify your pattern in love. Give up blaming anyone even yourself. Think about this and ask yourself "How have I been showing up in the relationships?" In what ways have you been clandestinely creating this experience? For instance, how often are you saying to yourself?

- "I only attract unavailable men"?
- "Men in my life always leave"?
- "I am never the one chosen"?

Once you recognize these thoughts, it becomes important to change those thoughts when they come to mind. Now that you are aware, when these thoughts come up you can replace unavailable with available, for example.

Completing Your Past You must complete the past in order to make room for a conscious committed love to come into your life. Here is a list of examples of what you may want to consider when determining what needs to be done in the area of completing your past.

- Old unsettled resentments
- Old agreements
- Toxic ties; toxic relational dynamics that are literally causing you to lose personal power and to show up as a lesser version of yourself
- Fear of obligation and/or commitment
- Guilt, and the inability to tell the truth and set proper boundaries

When it comes to completing the past, answer the following questions: How did you give your power to this person? How do you reclaim your power? This is completely of the past, process about completing all toxic relationships. That includes those you have with family, at work, and with friends. Checking to see what resentments you have to give up in order to stop being the victim. Remember, you can only control and change you.

Recognizing Core Love Beliefs Core Love Identity is transforming your core belief about what is possible or not possible when it comes to love. This is held at the level of identity, where how you identify with you and your very sense of self, your own value, your worthiness to love and be loved, and your thoughts of life and love are held. Here you may find beliefs like:

- Life doesn't support me to have love.
- I'm alone (men always leave me).
- I am invisible.
- I am not worthy.
- Relationships do not last.
- Marriage is a trap.

Once you recognize what your core belief about love is, you can then take the necessary steps to change that belief. This is going to require some work and change on your behalf. As with all exercises in this book, you will notice that everything is about you and steps that you will need to take, changes you will need to make. You will notice I will repeat this a lot: "you can only change you."

Practice: Bring yourself into awareness of that painful disappointing pattern that has been showing up over and over in your life. Imagine when the painful and disappointing moment happens, notice where this pain lands in your body. Close your eyes to get connected and breathe in that feeling. Welcome in the feeling and place hands on the part of the body where you can feel that pain being activated and breathe into that center. Allow yourself to get deeper and wiser (not about becoming the perfect person or resolving all your issues), breathing and welcoming in all these feelings.

Finding Your BLISS in the Midst of Pain

From that place you want to see if you can get to the emotional center of each feeling so that you can name what it is, like: "I am" or "I am NOT." If the emotion could tell you its name, for example - I am NOT important, I am NOT wanted, etc., this will assist in helping you accept the root belief at the core level. Allow yourself to feel and see the pain and belief as it is, so that you can stop it at the core.

4. Becoming magnetic to love. To become magnetic to the things you want to create:
   - Partner with the creative force, trust that the universe knows and hears you.
   - Turn attention toward you being the person you need to be in order to receive love in your life.
   - You must be willing to commit and willing to stand for the intentions that you have made when it comes to manifesting love.

Dr. Camelia Straughn

Remember you cannot force love. We have subconscious attracting. Focus on becoming that person you have the potential to be, who you would need to be in order to receive a great love in your life. Do not focus on the external, i.e., when or where do I find him or her. Yet focus on how to be magnetic to inspire the heavens and earth to move mountains to fulfill your intentions.

This is going to require from you a real commitment to begin to actively grow and evolve yourself into the person you would need to be not just to attract, but to also sustain, a great love over time.

You want to be making an unwavering commitment to do whatever it takes to cause your own evolution, your emancipation from patterns of the past. It is not just being interested in becoming the best version of yourself but also to really activate the magnetic field for a love to find you. You have to put your stake in the ground, you have to be standing and saying this shall be, I am standing for the future. Organizing your life around who you will need to be in order to fulfill upon your future. Do not allow yourself to be derailed or discouraged because, remember, this is a process. Part of this learning process will cause you to experience and have some mishaps and disappointments, know that.

It is going to be important that you truly function from the area of self-love and understand how it is important to have this as your foundation. Self-love is the organic foundation - you cannot receive or attract that which you cannot give to yourself. Become fully accountable for your life.

Dr. Camelia Straughn

NOTES

CHAPTER 3 – Key 2

INTIMACY – IN 2 ME I SEE

Dr. Camelia Straughn

When you ask a person to tell you what they think of when they hear, read, or even say the word intimacy, they immediately begin to speak about sex or some physical connection. In reality, when we look deep into this word and the concept of intimacy, we find words like closeness, knowledge, caring, and interdependence. I know you are asking yourself, "How is understanding intimacy going to move you to *BLISS* when there always seems to be a plethora of memories and circumstances where pain is at the forefront of the situation?" One will first need to understand the different levels and categories of intimacy. This understanding comes from a close examination of the levels and yourself - seeing, recognizing, and accepting your part in the creation of pain in this and every area of your life, and doing this without blaming.

Finding Your BLISS in the Midst of Pain

Honesty with yourself is going to be key as you work through each level. Seeing how you view it and what your behaviors and thoughts are at each level is paramount. Not only honesty, but also recognizing the part you play in not being where you want to be is also key. Understanding this is not about blaming. Rather, it is about recognizing that we all are responsible for our lives as they are and as we want them to be.

When one really looks at the concept of intimacy it can be a little overwhelming. It is my hope that as you work through this section of the book, you will be able to grasp a clear understanding of intimacy at every level - more specifically, how you as an individual see yourself at each level, and who you are sharing that level with. Now, there five levels of intimacy and six categories that we as human beings experience as we move and navigate through this journey called life.

It is understood that intimacy is the degree to which a person can share feelings with another in any relationship. As you are working this chapter, I want you to also look at and contemplate how you apply the concepts of intimacy to yourself, as it is important in order to find BLISS in the midst of pain.

This is critical because before you can ever experience a healthy intimate relationship with another you must have a good and healthy relationship with yourself. Do you trust your own advice and do you like spending time with yourself? The answer to these and many more self-related questions are going to be important to ask and answer. And remember, it's just you, so be true and free with your answers. This is the only way you will be able to invoke change and move forward.

In looking at the definition of intimacy we find

that it is considered a place of closeness. This closeness is linked to commitment, satisfaction, passion, love, support and positive regard. What better way to master intimacy and to experience all the relational connection than with yourself?

Intimacy is something I like to call "into me I see." How wonderful is it to take this commonly misunderstood and misused word and apply it only to you. This will allow you to build a complete healthy regard for yourself. This healthy regard will better assist you in getting an understanding of what you want and most importantly what you need. Coming to terms with your deepest desires. All while realizing that all is good.

FIVE LEVELS OF INTIMACY

Psychologists have identified five levels of emotional intimacy we all move through as we get to know someone. It is important to note that intimacy is really at the core about communication. So you will notice at each level we will focus on how communication happens at each level. They've been given many names, but for our purposes, let's call them Level One through Five, with five being the highest, or most intimate level. I want to make sure that you are clear, beloved, that some relationships will not go to, nor will they need to go to, Level Five. Yet, some will go to various degrees or conditions, if you will. Meaning you can take each level in its conceptual form and apply it to your work environment, school environment, and religious environment. In doing so, look at who and why do you allow the different people in these groups to operate with you on each of the different levels.

Level One: Safe Communication

Finding Your BLISS in the Midst of Pain

Level One is the lowest level of communication. We call it safe because it simply involves the exchange of facts and information. Level One does not require any feelings, opinions, or personal vulnerability and therefore is no risk of rejection. This is the kind of interaction we have with people we don't know well. **It's the chitchat we share with the clerk at the grocery store or a stranger at a party.** People communicating at this level share minimal intimacy. An example of this level would be, "Lousy weather we're having," "This is great pizza," or "My team won last night." It may become clear that it is best to interact with people you have known for some time only at this level, and know that this is okay.

Level Two: Others' Opinions and Beliefs

At Level Two, we start sharing other people's

thoughts, beliefs, and opinions. We are beginning to reveal more of ourselves through our associations. We say things like, "My mother always says…" or "One of my favorite authors said…" When we use these statements, it is our way of testing the other person's reaction to what we're sharing without offering our own opinions. This is slightly more vulnerable than Level One, but because we're not sharing our own opinions we **can distance ourselves from the opinion if we feel threatened** by criticism or rejection. This level gives us more of an out when having connecting conversations with others.

Level Three: Personal Opinions and Beliefs

In associating with others at Level Three, we start taking small risks. At this level, we begin to share our own thoughts, opinions, and beliefs. But unlike in the previous level, if we begin feeling too vulnerable, **we say we've switched our opinions or changed our mind in order to avoid conflict or pain.** I think at this point it would be a great time to point out that moving through these levels is also a confirmation of whether or not a person or group can be trusted in our opinion.

Level Four: My Feelings and Experiences

Sharing feelings and experiences is the next level of vulnerability and intimacy. At this level, we talk about our joys, pain, and failures; our mistakes in the past, our dreams, and our goals; what we like or don't like. What makes us who we are? **This level is more vulnerable because we can't change how we feel about something or the details of our past or current experiences.** If we sense that we may be rejected or criticized, all we can do is try to convince others that we are no longer impacted by our past. We are no longer that person. We are different now. We will also remind the person that we shared this information because we trust them, not to be judged.

Level Five: My Needs, Emotions and Desires

Level Five is the highest level of intimacy. It is the level where we are known at the deepest core of who we are. Because of that, it is the level that requires the greatest amount of trust. **If I cannot trust that you won't reject me, I'll never be able to share my deepest self with you.** Unlike the other levels, there is **no escape at this level**. Once I let someone see who I really am, I can no longer convince them otherwise. Communicating at this level means we offer someone the most vulnerable part of ourselves. The greatest fear is that they could use it against us later. When we share things like, "I'm hurt when you do not call," I need to feel respected by you," or "I want to spend my life with you," we are sharing not only our hurts but our desires and needs as well. It is also the level where we let others see our emotional reaction to things, which if you are like me, is not always a pretty sight. Maybe that is why we save those for the ones closest to us, like our families and significant other.

SIX FORMS OF INTIMACY

The first form of intimacy is cognitive or intellectual intimacy, where two people exchange thoughts, share ideas, and enjoy similarities and differences between their opinions. This form of intimacy also involves a mutual understanding; you have created a safe place to have discussion within your relationship. If you can do this in an open and comfortable way, then you can become quite intimate in the intellectual area. Simply put, intellectual intimacy can be defined as sharing ideas, issues or concerns, or philosophy based on mutual respect for each other's intellect and education.

A second form of intimacy is experiential intimacy, intimacy activity, or recreational intimacy. This is simply being together. Some ways to participate in experiential intimacy would be where people get together to actively involve themselves with each other. During this time, they are saying very little to each other, not sharing any thoughts or many feelings, but being involved in mutual activities with one another. Intimacy in this form would also be taking a walk together, going to the museum, hiking a mountain, or my personal favorite cooking dinner together. Consider this, imagine observing two house painters whose brushstrokes seemed to be playing out a duet on the side of a house. You, as well as they, may be shocked to think that they were engaged in an intimate activity with each other. However, from an experiential point of view, they would be very intimately involved.

A third form of intimacy is emotional intimacy where two persons can comfortably share their feelings with each other or when they empathize with the feelings of the other person. When one really tries to understand and tries to be aware of the other person's emotional side. Emotional intimacy can be expressed both verbally and nonverbally. Emotional Intimacy is an aspect of interpersonal relationships that varies in intensity from relationship to another and varies from on time to another.

A fourth form of intimacy is spiritual intimacy. Spiritual intimacy is the process of profoundly connecting the core of one's being to another without giving up one's own self. Shared religious beliefs and observed religious practices come together between you and your mate, such as praying together, going to religious services together, or discussing spiritual concerns and issues as a couple.

A fifth form of intimacy is financial intimacy. Financial intimacy is the sharing of your financial situation. In this form of intimacy, you and your partner will develop plans for your finances and will have communications about your finances and other money matters that are open and honest. It is very important that one is aware of the financial condition when one is part of a marriage or domestic living situation.

A sixth form of intimacy is sexual (physical) intimacy. Physical intimacy is sensual closeness or touching. It is an act or reaction, such as expression of feelings between people. Physical intimacy includes

- but is not limited to - love making, being inside someone's personal space, holding hands, hugging, kissing, and caressing. This is the stereotypical definition of intimacy that most people are familiar with. However, this form of intimacy includes a broad range of sensuous activity and is much more than just sexual intercourse. It's any form of sensual expression with each other. Therefore, physical intimacy can be many things for different people at different times. We humans were designed to want to be touched, and it is a very important part of our growth and our sense of belonging and feeling loved.

Dr. Camelia Straughn

NOTES

CHAPTER 4 – Key 3

FAITH

Dr. Camelia Straughn

Know that work and struggle must take place for the wisdom to come. Never lose faith. You may lose wealth, health, and even people. But faith is going to be your cornerstone of success. Never lose sight of your goal, faith and belief that the Creator has not left you alone. This process must happen to draw you near to the Creator. Hold fast to your consciousness realizing that the earth belongs to the Creator. As odd as this sounds, your soul needs a good challenge, a good fight or a worthy opponent of sorts; this is how you grow. And what greater opponent is there than the Life Journey?

Remember this as you reflect on the challenges you face. Instead of focusing on your frustration, try to focus on the spiritual lessons that you are learning from your challenges. The lesson might be courage, self-love, or forgiveness. Sometimes the lesson is drastic - that is time to cut some people loose and move on with your life.

It is important to understand this concept called faith. Faith is complete trust in someone or something. It is being sure of the things that we hope for and knowing that something is real even when we do not see it. What are some things that you can do to strengthen or improve your faith? This is going to be a very personal task, meaning that like many of the tasks in this book, it will require that you look inside of you and make conscious decisions to act, respond, and behave differently.

Trust unconditionally that the Creator will give you the how. Begin where you are and with what you have and move forward. Beloved, it is important to remember and recognize that faith has nothing to do with doctrine or belief. What do I mean by this? What

I mean is that your religion or even your belief that there is a higher power does not guarantee that you will have faith or even practice it. Faith equals trust unquestioned, unconditional trust in the Creator. That is it. Trusting that the Creator will provide for and protect you. True faith is primarily demonstrated by actions - our life - not described by our words.

Let us note, that it is important to recognize that Faith Is Action. So, I asked what level or standard of faith are you in? In my research and study of several religions I found that for all general purposes there are three levels or stages of faith. Which brings me to a quick sidebar and that is we have more similarities than differences. Now to get back to the subject at hand and that is the level or stages of faith.

Level One is where you have little faith. This stage is characterized by struggling to believe the

Finding Your BLISS in the Midst of Pain

Creator. You hope the Creator will answer your prayer but you just are not sure. Sometimes doubt creeps in because you are looking at your circumstance or situation not at the Creator or maybe your problem is that you just do not know what the Creator has said (in the word) so you have nothing on which to anchor your faith. This is where one says, "I will believe it when I see it."

Level Two is great faith. This stage involves stretching to believe the Creator more and more. At this level you are beginning to stand on the truth of Scripture. Note this scripture can come from a gamete of when you let the words of the Creator shape your thinking and petitions, you know that the Creator will grant your request. At this level, you are beginning to understand the concept, "when I believe I will see."

Level Three is perfect faith. When you are

walking at this level you are resting in the confidence that the Creator has already accomplished what you have asked for. Knowing and understanding that when your requests are in line with the Creator's will it is a done deal. Your job is to simply thank the Creator and watch the promise become a reality. At this level, you have to know and trust the concept, "when I believe, I will see." So you begin with believing, no matter the circumstance.

Be assured that no matter where you are, the Creator wants you to continually progress. Take a moment and take a look at where you are with your faith. You do not find because you do not seek, you do not have because you do not ask and the door does not open because you do not knock. Faith is about action, because without action, faith is dead. Be willing to take an honest look at yourself and have a willingness to change and to take action that will allow you to walk at the highest level of faith which will assure you that everything works out for your good.

Dr. Camelia Straughn

NOTES

CHAPTER 5 - Key 4

FORGIVENESS

Dr. Camelia Straughn

I put the letter on my desk, wiped the tears from my face, and just sat there wondering how one person experiences this type of betrayal before age twenty. This woman who was no longer twenty had just revealed to me how she had been raped and molested from the age of five until she was seventeen years old. In turn, she got married before twenty and her husband physically, emotionally, and sexually abused her. She talked about how her life had been one horrible relationship after another and just wanted to know when it would stop. She talked about the fact that she had resolved and become ok with being alone for the rest of her life on this earth. As I read her letter I could hear the pain and anger that she was still experiencing and holding on to even though she was now 45.

When Kathy walked into my office, she stood

tall and walked with the confidence of a runway model. She was beautiful, not just by nature's standards (for every created life is beautiful in its own right), but also by those set by society. The truth is, I was really surprised, and her letter had painted her as a total victim, so much so that I was looking for it to have made a physical appearance. Again, I was prepared to meet a woman who was not only broken but who also looked broken.

After Kathy told me her story again, and believe me, she told it with an even greater level of anger, passion, and pain than she did when she wrote me. She also revealed that she had attempted to suicide several times in her life. When she stopped talking, I asked her what is it that that she thought was the reason that the suicides were not successful. Her answer was surprising to me and brought me relief. She said "my desire to die was not stronger than my desire to not allow them to know that they broke me." Inside I was jumping for joy; Kathy wanted to live and she wanted to be free from the pain and anger of the lifelong betrayal.

I knew that she was ready to receive the information that was going to take her to the next level of her healing. I also recognized that it may not be easy. She had lived this life of making sure that no one knew what had happened to her. So it was going to be important to help her to not be ashamed of her experiences, her story. During our conversations I introduced Kathy to the concept of forgiving the men who had molested her when she was a child and to forgive the men who had abused her as a woman as well. To forgive her mother, who she had held responsible for the pain and hurt she experienced as a child. This was hard for her to grasp because she really believed that these were acts that were not forgivable. Not only that, she had to get past the anger she felt for herself, for she held herself totally responsible for the abuse she experienced as an adult woman. And so the journey to forgiveness began!

Forgiveness is necessary for healing and nothing is unforgivable. Forgiveness of others is essential to mental peace and radiant health. You must forgive everyone who has ever hurt you, including yourself if you want perfect health and happiness. Holding onto anger is like drinking poison and expecting the other person to die.

Please note, in the forgiveness process, we have more than people to forgive. We have to forgive the thoughts, beliefs, and behaviors attached to that experience as well as what people have done. The way to practice forgiveness is to write it, speak it, and say it whenever you experience judgment or get upset. Forgiveness is not about forgetting; you may never forget what was said or did to you. You will however, gain greater clarity and strength about how you allow the experience to affect you. In the forgiveness process you have to begin to let go of the thought and idea that someone is obligated to tell you sorry or someone else should pay for what happened to you. I want you to begin to operate in the arena of true love and peace.

The first step of forgiveness is to forgive yourself. In most instances, we are not always upset or angry with others; we are really angry with ourselves. We are angry that we allowed these things to happen to us. We get caught up in the thought that if I had made a different decision, things would be different. Maybe so, but this cannot be your lifelong focus. So the healing begins with you. When the anger or chaos rises up, stop and say I forgive myself. You have to let go of the anger and the

Finding Your BLISS in the Midst of Pain

chaos. Know that letting go of anger and pain does not mean denying or stuffing our anger and pain. Doing that will cause you to be tired and bitter.

Forgiveness is a process of purification, the purification of mind and spirit and freeing, if you will. There is a book I want you to consider reading, *The Power of Your Subconscious Mind* by Dr. Joseph Murphy. I will share with you a very effective forgiveness technique. This technique will show you and allow you to bring about forgiveness in yourself, for yourself and others. You will notice I will refer to this technique as Forgiveness Treatment practice. Forgiveness Treatment will work wonders in your life. It will create a wonderful sense of peace and comfort. The key is going to be to do it!

When going into this practice I want you to quiet your mind, relax and let go. To think of the Creator's love for you and then affirm "I fully and freely forgive (think of the name of the offender). I release him or her mentally and spiritually. I completely forgive everything connected with the matter in question. I am free and he/she is free. It is a marvelous feeling. This is my day of amnesty. I release anybody who has ever hurt me and I wish for each and everyone health, happiness, and peace, and I do this freely, joyously, and lovingly.

Whenever I think of the person or persons who hurt me, I say, "I have released you, and all the blessings of life are yours. I am free and you are free. It is wonderful." I know it may seem like a lot but nothing is as freeing as truly forgiving those who have wronged us and letting go of the pain. The great secret and the beautiful thing about true forgiveness is that once you have forgiven the person, it is not necessary to repeat the prayer or do the Forgiveness Treatment as it pertains to that particular person or experience. This does not mean that you may not have thoughts of the person or that you will be instantly detached from the experience. What it does mean is that you can move forward without the experience controlling your thoughts and or emotions. So when the person or a particular hurt happens to come to mind, wish the individual well and say, "I release you and peace be unto you."

Remember this is a technique and process. Do this as often as the thought comes to your mind, and you will notice that after a few days (for some a few weeks), the thought of the person and the experience will come to mind less and less often until it literally fades into nothingness. It is important to be kind and gentle with yourself as you work through the Forgiveness Treatment, know that this is your journey and do not allow others to dictate how fast you move from one stage to the other. However, it is important to keep moving forward.

Now, how do you know when you have truly forgiven? Well, there's a simple acid test. Just imagine me coming to you and telling you something wonderful about the person who wronged you, cheated you, or defrauded you. Now, what comes to mind? Do you cringe at hearing the good news about the person? If this is the case, then the seeds of hurt and anger are still in your subconscious mind trying to take root and wreak havoc on you.

The simple truth about forgiveness is that you remember the incident but you will no longer feel the hurt or the sting of it. Again, the forgiveness of others is essential to your mental peace and health. It is imperative and a must, in fact, for you to forgive everyone who has ever hurt you regardless of how trivial it may seem.

If you want perfect health and happiness,

Finding Your BLISS in the Midst of Pain

forgive yourself by getting your thoughts in harmony with divine law and order. To refuse to forgive yourself is nothing but spiritual pride and ignorance. I'm sure at this point you're asking what all this means, or why is it important anyway. Here's the thing: once you understand the power of your subconscious mind and the creative law of your own mind, you will no longer blame others and conditions for making or marring your life. Listen Beautiful One, forgiveness is about getting your thoughts in line with divine law of harmony. The one thing you may want to consider and recognize is that self-condemnation is called hell, bondage, and restriction while the other side is forgiveness and is called heaven, harmony, and peace.

I know you may be thinking, 'What is she talking about, is she really serious?' and yes I am, very serious. When you allow past decisions and hurtful behaviors of others to hold your emotions hostage you are living a life of hell. Yet, when you open your heart up to forgiveness, your life resembles that peace and harmony that we envision heaven to be.

Finally, forgiveness is accepting that something "WRONG" has happened to you. It is not accepting that it was OK that it happened. It is letting go of the past. Letting go of the past we thought we wanted. Releasing negative perception of it and coming to the PRESENT. Giving up the hope or idea that the past could be anything or any different than it actually was. Letting go so that the past does not hold you prisoner, so that it does not hold you hostage. As you end your forgiveness treatments, pray for guidance and right action. Take what comes and realize it is good and very good knowing there is no cause for self-pity, criticism, or hatred. Remember Kathy? Well

Finding Your BLISS in the Midst of Pain

we met at a conference a few months after our session, and I could tell that her spirit was free of the pain and anger. Most importantly, she knew and she now lives in the beauty of forgiveness.

Dr. Camelia Straughn

NOTES

NOTES

Dr. Camelia Straughn

CHAPTER 6 - Key 5

SELF-CARE

Finding Your BLISS in the Midst of Pain

What do you mean by take time for me? It was as if Cynthia was angry with me, because she could not see the importance of self-care. Cynthia began to tell me the list of things that she was responsible for in the course of a day. Then she began to inform me of the things that she had to complete within the week. She spoke with such passion that she had almost convinced me that the time that she was taking to meet with me was causing her not to be able to get everything done. At this point, I literally had to stop her! She had worked herself into a frenzy of such magnitude that if I allowed her to continue, we both would begin to believe that self-care for her was useless and a waste of time and not possible.

I reminded Cynthia of how her life had spiraled out of control before our sessions started. Reminding her of how much more receptive she had become to her children and her husband since the beginning. I then had her to list all the things that had improved since she started blocking out the times on a weekly basis for us to meet. This session was about taking everything to the next level. It was time for Cynthia to really start to make personal time for herself (outside of our sessions). I reminded her that self-care is essential for her survival.

Self-care is something that most of us do not even think about and those of us who do, we rarely make it a consistent part of our daily life. You must be good to yourself if you're going to be any good to others. This means to take a day off once in awhile when it is not scheduled, eat a piece of chocolate when it's not recommended, take a nap when it seems it is just not possible, get your face in a good book for an hour when you cannot afford to, soak in a tub when there is no time to, stop everything when you are not supposed to. Do this now, right now for goodness sake!

What is self-care you ask? Self-care is exactly what it implies - care provided for you by you. It is about identifying your own needs and taking steps to meet them. It is taking the time to do some of the activities that nurture you. Self-care is about taking proper care of yourself and treating yourself as kindly as you treat others. It is about understanding, knowing and accepting the concept of rest. When most of us think of self-care, especially women, we convince ourselves that it is a selfish act and that by taking time for ourselves we are somehow neglecting our family. Even more devastating is that the women who believe that self-care means selfishness will try to impose that thought on those who have made self-care a part of their lives. Nothing could be further from the truth. Don't believe me? Think on this: when you go on a flight, the flight attendant explains all of the safety precautions. Then, when at the part about the oxygen mask, the attendant begins to explain the importance of putting your mask on First, even if you are traveling with a small child. Self-care is putting on that oxygen mask dropping down in front of you. If you do not put yours on first (before you help anyone else), you are going to die, and most likely before you get a mask on your child who would likely die as well. So it stands to reason that in order to take better care of your family you must take care of you.

    The concept of self-care goes into looking at the need to rest. Now, this rest does not specifically or only mean sleep, but is related to the concept of restoration. When you rest, you are replenished or you receive back those things that have been expended or put out. If you do not rest there's no restoration. If you do not restore, then you have nothing else to give. Rest is a form of calmness; it allows you to listen to spirit so that you are not always working on the problem(s). I like to use this analogy for my clients and I will share with you: prayer is talking to the Creator; meditation/rest is listening to the Creator. We need to spend more time listening. Let us make this clear, sometimes it is going to take work just to find the place of rest and calm. This simply means that you have to take an active part in making sure that you rest so that you can be restored. This time of rest and calm can be taken by setting aside five to ten minutes daily so as to just get quiet. As you make this rest time a part of your day, do not get distracted by what you are supposed to be doing. In the beginning, your thoughts are going to be all over the place and that is

OK, just breathe. Know that as you grow and evolve your mind will begin to quiet itself. Also as you grow you will want to increase this time of rest. This technique of self-care is something that I would suggest that you make a permanent part of your daily life. We like to refer to this time as meditating, something that has changed my life and my perspective on it and my purpose in it.

Another form of self-care is understanding the need to stay grounded. Have you or do you ever feel like you are not fully in your body; you feel a bit floaty or you are less able to manage the practicalities of your life than usual, you may need to activate your base chakra by grounding yourself. The base Chakra is all about survival, instincts, and stability. The Base Chakra or Root Chakra is located at the base of the spine and controls the energy for kinesthetic feeling and movement. It is the foundation of physical energy and spiritual energy for the body. Now, if this concept of chakra is new to you, I would suggest that you do something as simple as a "Google" search or maybe research some books on it.

I will tell you that there are seven chakra levels. From bottom to top: Root Chakra, Sacral Chakra, Solar Plexus, Heart Chakra, Throat Chakra, Third Eye and Crown Chakra. At the end of the chapter, I have put a diagram to show how this relates to the body.

Some quick ways to ground yourself are to:
- Walk barefoot on the grass or earth
- Visualize that you have roots growing from your feet and like a tree you are planted to the earth
- Stand approximately twenty inches in front of a wall, with your back to the wall bend your knees and lean back until your back is pressing

against the wall and your feet pressing into the ground hold this position for a couple of minutes and feel the energy pulsing in your legs grounding you.

Along with incorporating this quiet time and grounding exercise, you can also try taking a bath once per week. During this time you can also incorporate getting quiet while cleansing your body. You can also add your favorite essential oils to your bath. Another form of self-care that some women find difficult to employ is simply saying "no." Allowing yourself to be ok and give yourself permission to say "no" is paramount. Believe me this was a hard one to learn. So be kind to yourself. Regardless to what you have been conditioned to believe you cannot do everything and it is not smart to try. You cannot be everywhere nor can you be everything to everyone and again it is not smart to try.

Finding Your BLISS in the Midst of Pain

Finally, learn to set your mental default to happy. This does that mean you will not have moments of time of unhappiness or frustration but this will allow you to shorten the time that you are in those moments. I know you may be wondering what happened to Cynthia. Well, the journey continues. She has really started to embrace the beauty in our sessions and she is working on saying "no," because for her it will allow her to implement the other strategies of self-care.

Dr. Camelia Straughn

NOTES

CHAPTER 7 - Key 6

EMPOWERMENT

Dr. Camelia Straughn

In this chapter, we will talk about self-empowerment. I have collected some motivating quotes and phrases for you to copy, memorize (if you like), and post in your cubicle at work, on your mirror in your bathroom, and on the refrigerator. Use these quotes to remind you that every trial and circumstance is about a lesson that needs to be learned and will facilitate your growth. We define self-empowerment as deriving the strength to do something through one's own thoughts and based on the belief that you know what is best for you.

You have been introduced to many techniques and processes that will allow you to live an extraordinary life. As you work through making these processes a part of your daily life, and begin to receive and accept the benefits of them, you will see that it is all about trusting yourself. Knowing that you are responsible for you and, regardless of what is and has happened, you know what will work for you. Remember that this is your life and you are the one living it, so make it a great one. What have you done and more importantly what have you said to yourself about your life and where you are right now?

The question now will be what you can do to become self-empowered. One of the first things I am going to suggest you do is to really examine what it is you say to yourself whenever you are met with an obstacle in your life. It is not what happens to you; it is how you react internally to what is happening. In order for this chapter to be of any value you it will be important to take time to begin to know how you talk to yourself. Do you know that the way you talk to yourself will create your feelings and emotions and eventually establish your actions? The goal is to learn and develop an effective and positive way to talk to yourself and in doing this you will have more control in every aspect of your life.

Now Beloved, I want you to think about a time when you were meet with an obstacle in your life, what did you say to yourself? It is very important to note the words you used to describe the situation, because it will determine the quality and tone of your emotional life. It is important to begin to see things in a more positive and constructive way. Always seeking for the good in any situation, you will begin to be more positive and optimistic and more likely to learn the lesson the first time. Begin thinking of what you want, and keep your mind off of what you do not want or what you fear (false evidence appearing real).

We understand that in life we are always faced with challenges and problems this is unavoidable.

Finding Your BLISS in the Midst of Pain

But, if you treat every problem and challenge as an opportunity to grow yourself and respond by taking action in learning what the lesson is you will always grow and learn. You will become a stronger and better version of your greater self. In practicing positive self-talk, you should keep your words and mental visualization consistent with your goals and targets, in doing this there is nothing that can stop you from the success you believe you are meant to have.

Here are few affirmations that you can read and refer back to from time to time. It is important to know how great and powerful you are.

I heard Les Brown give a speech one day, and I felt like out of everyone in the room, he was talking directly to me. He said, "So, you have taken a big hit, life has knocked you down; but you are not knocked out. You have more going for you than you realize.

Others might laugh and say you are through. But, they do not know you like that. You have the ability to pull victory from the jaws of defeat. Now is the time for you to gather your wits, clear your mind, dig down deep, and resolve to unleash your creative energy, unstoppable attitude and resourcefulness. This is your time and your moment to prove to yourself and everyone else who you really are. You have the power to open the doors of possibility and move your life forward. You have the power within you, because you have something special, you have greatness within you." So, now I tell it to you. "You have the power within you, because you have something special, you have greatness within you."

"We look for happiness in relationship and when we do not find it we think something is wrong with the relationship. What is wrong is the belief that relationships are the source of happiness or empowerment. Know that you are the source of your happiness. Remember to tell yourself 'I embrace this opportunity to be better than I was yesterday, I take responsibility for my choices today and always.'" – Camelia Straughn

"You may encounter many defeats but you must not be defeated, in fact it may be necessary to encounter the defeats so you can know who you are, what you can rise from and how you can still come out of it." - Maya Angelou

FEAR - **F**alse **E**vidence **A**ppearing **R**eal! Fear wears so many clever disguises it is virtually impossible to always recognize it. Fear disguises itself as the need to be somewhere else doing something else, not knowing how to do something or not needing to do something. Do not be afraid of change because it is leading you to a new beginning.

Most of you (me included) can give up something that you do not like. When it comes to giving up things that you like you, will not do it, thinking you are going to miss something or lose something. This is what is holding you back. Being able to practice perfect surrender. Perfect surrender is when you give up everything, including your body to the Creator. Telling the Creator, "Do what You want with me, do what You want with my body, mind, with my affairs with everything; not my will but Thine." If you can surrender like this, you are already free. Try it. It is hard, because you are afraid of what will happen after you do that. You believe everything will be taken away from you. This is human thinking, stop being human, surrender yourself to become totally free." – Robert Adams

"There is nothing I have to do, there is no where I have to go, and no way I have to be except exactly the way I am being right now. My happiness is knowing this, my joy is expressing this, my bliss is experiencing it." – Camelia Straughn

"Life is not an accident. Your story is not an accident. You are here for a divine reason. You are someone's miracle. You are someone's blessing. You are someone's breakthrough. You are someone's second chance. You are someone's example. That's why you are next in line for a miracle. You are not an accident." – Les Brown

"You cannot stay where you are and get to where you are going. Surrender, some things are not worth holding onto any longer." – Camelia Straughn

Dr. Camelia Straughn

"There is no need for you to be some type of super human being in order to measure up to everyone else. Who you are is really quite enough. You know enough, you have enough to offer something valuable to whatever is going on." – Camelia Straughn

"Study your seeds instead of your needs. You will never be in a place where you have nothing. Learn to plant your seeds instead of eating them." – Meleshi Crawford (QueenCode)

"Remember that the mind is a wonderful servant but a horrible master. Stop allowing your mind to bully you." - Camelia Straughn

NOTES

CHAPTER 8 - Key 7

EMBRACING YOU

Finding Your BLISS in the Midst of Pain

I had been working with Ann for about six months and she had made great strides in accomplishing all the goals that she had set for herself. Still, she found herself struggling with her weight. Now, I know you are thinking - well that is no big deal every woman is struggling with her weight. In all fairness, I would agree with that statement.

The problem was that Ann had come to a great balance when it came to her eating habits and her workouts. But she could not reach her goal weight. So, we began to have really deep conversations about what she saw when she looked in the mirror. I mean who did she really see? As the conversation continued, it dawned on me that Ann would always refer to herself as chunky. It became clear that she would forever be on this rollercoaster as long as she could not see herself at a healthy weight.

So we began to work on how she talked to herself as it pertained to her weight. I explained to her, that her words have power and they will build you up or break you down. It was going to be her choice as to what would happen. It was exciting to watch her grasp this, because she had seen how it made a difference in the other areas of her life, so it was not hard to get her to consider making the adjustment. The challenge was that she had gotten so comfortable with degrading herself when it came to her weight that it took some doing to even recognize the triggers and then switch her thoughts and the words she was using to describe herself. The great thing is that Ann became committed to making change when it came to how she talked to herself, and began to see a change in her weight in all of eight weeks.

Finding Your BLISS in the Midst of Pain

You are the source, everything you need is within you! Your light is seen. Your heart is known. Your soul is cherished by more people than you might imagine. If you knew how many others have been touched in wonderful ways by you, you would be astonished. If you knew how many people feel so much for you, you would be shocked. You are more wonderful than you think you are. Rest with that. Rest easy with that. Breathe again. You are doing fine, more than fine you're doing great! So relax and love yourself today! Remember positive energy carries a higher vibration, operate in that because it will bring blessings to you quicker! Always go where you are celebrated, not where you are tolerated.

In this chapter we really take a deeper look into who we really are. Have you wondered who you truly are? Let's be real, for most of us we are hindered by what we see in the mirror. Remember Ann and how she kept perpetuating that image, the image she did not like, simply through the words that she was speaking to herself? We get caught up in the Hollywood definition of beauty and success. So we begin to beat ourselves up when we do not meet those standards. The ironic thing is that what we do not realize is that they are doing the same thing to themselves. Beloved, here's the deal: I want you to make a commitment to yourself and embrace your flaws and accept yourself completely. Here are ten tips for you to apply to every flaw that you believe you have.

1. Acknowledge what's bothering you. The significance of this is to get and understanding and get to the root of your concerns. Without understanding, you cannot come to terms with your flaws. I want you to dig deep and see if there are any

issues beneath the flaws that you need to address. In most instances it is the underlying issues that are actually the problem. Complaining or focusing on a flaw is really just a cover up for the real issue. So dig deep and acknowledge.

2. Use your flaws to guide self-improvement. Let's be clear - embracing your flaws does not mean you cannot improve yourself. In most cases the flaws we recognize gives us the opportunity to work on those imperfections. Remember, if you want to change something about yourself then go for it, do it. You do not need anyone's permission. The caveat to this is to be sure the change is not based on self-hate or someone else's standard.

3. Appreciate your individuality. The amazing thing about flaws is that they are what makes us different

from everyone else. Yes, it is your choice to change anything about yourself that you do not like. But I will suggest that you do not try to fit the mold. Just imagine how boring the world would be if we all had the same gifts, talent, look, were the same height etc. Just look at all the people who did alter some part of them that they considered a flaw and before long, they came to regret it. So, be careful that does not become you.

4. Do not let your flaws hold you back. I'm going to suggest that you look up the TLC reality show Abby and Brittany. I do not normally watch TV especially reality TV, but I wanted you to have an example that would bring this tip home. Abby and Brittany are conjoined twins with parents who raised them to believe they can do anything anyone else can do, and, they do. Now, I know that there is a possibility

that you did not come from a supportive environment and that is OK. Because you can choose how your day, life for that matters goes. Think about how different your life could be, would be if you did as Abby and Brittany did embrace your difference and get on with life. Think on that!

5. Put things in perspective. Now I want you to take a piece of paper and write down five things that you are grateful for. On the other side I want you to write down five things that would improve if you were a stunning beauty and look at how they weigh in. Once compared to what you are grateful for, I'm sure that you would rather have your health, beauty, and family over any temporary improvement that being a stunning beauty would bring.

6. Make your flaws famous! All this means is stop

body shaming. Case in point, slogans such as "real women have curves" are just as detrimental to someone's self-esteem as the plethora of size 0 models we are bombarded with every day. Body shaming can also manifest itself as criticizing your own appearance through a judgment or in comparison to another person. (e.g.,, "I'm so ugly compared to her." "Look at how broad my shoulders are."); criticizing another's appearance in front of them, (e.g., "With those thighs, you're never going to find a date."); criticizing another's appearance without their knowledge. (e.g., "Did you see what she's wearing today? Not flattering." "At least you don't look like *her*!"). If we want to reach a point of acceptance within ourselves, we also need to find beauty and acceptance in others. Plus, you always feel better when you are being positive.

7. Google it! For most of us we get stuck on not looking like the girl in the magazine. So, here's what I want you to do, Google it, yes, that's right. Type fat thighs or big nose in the search box insert images. Warning you will see some extreme images some digitally altered but I guarantee it will put things in perspective.

8. Flip your flaw! This is finding strength in your flaw, doing this will allow you to own it. Consider this, if you see yourself as shy and quiet that will most likely mean you are great at listening and an amazing observer.

9. Do not compare yourself! I want you to commit to the idea that this is your decade. This is the decade of you! Stop comparing yourself to others and love yourself for who you are - the Good, the Bad and the

Ugly. Remember everyone has their own idiosyncrasies that is what makes life so interesting.

10. Be flawsome. I know, I know but yes, flawsome is an actual term. Trendsetting.com coined it to describe brands that show humanity by being open about our flaws. In their words "human nature dictates that people have a hard time genuinely connecting with, being close to or really trusting other humans who pretend to have no weaknesses, flaws or mistakes." Who wants that? Embrace your flaws and be forever flawsome.

To complete this chapter here are a few mantras I want you to try. First, breathe in and breathe out slowly, then repeat:
- "The universe will provide what I need, when I need it"

- "I trust myself."

- "I trust the universe. I trust the Creator."

- "I love and accept myself for who I am."

- "I am healthy in body and spirit."

Take a moment to try one and see how it feels then choose the one you believe in and repeat it daily (sometimes several times daily).

Dr. Camelia Straughn

NOTES

CHAPTER 9 - Key 8

FASTING

Dr. Camelia Straughn

I know when you looked at the title of this chapter you initial thought was "oh, no" she is going to tell me how and what to eat. Be assured that is not the case. It is and always will be my intent that I will share information and what you do with it is your choice. So with that all being said, let's discuss this thing called fasting.

In this chapter we will discuss the concept or practice of fasting and how it will assist you both spiritually and physically. There are several types of fast. There is the cabbage fast, water fast, fruit juice fast and the lemonade fast etc. Most of us are more familiar with the religious (spiritual) fast. The inner workings of the religious fast will usually depend upon one religion. Please note we are discussing fasting as a spiritual and physical benefit. The religious take on it is for you to evaluate on your own.

Finding Your BLISS in the Midst of Pain

Fasting is a way to renew yourself, and cleanses your body of unknown toxins. Remember fasting is a very personal process/act and only you determine how detailed that process will be for you. So when you fast it is most beneficial to fast alone and show no one you are fasting. The Creator will see it and reward you greatly. Now for some there will be a time when coming together as a group for support and solidarity is important. Know that these are powerful and necessary. Although, even in these instances, it is important to make it about the group or the actual goal of the fast and not reminding people how great you are because you are fasting. After fasting the body has cleansed the blood of decaying, diseased cells, clogging waste and toxins, after which healthy cells are built of better material to replace those that were casted out of the body during the fast. Again, fasting is a great way to regenerate the mind, body and spirit.

Our leaders, masters, and healers recognized fasting as a great corrective or remedial measure and utilized it in instances of illness. Fasting twice in the week was a common custom in the days of Jesus. The disciples of John fasted often. David fasted 40 days as did Jesus. Gandhi fasted to the get the British out of India. Prophet Mohammed (pbuh) taught the Muslims to fast for 30 days once a year. These leaders knew to promote health and prolong life and free themselves from bondage of any and all kinds and they did it via fasting. A beautiful concept to consider is that all religions/faiths share the belief in promoting/practicing fasting and praying. In doing this deliberately it will allow you to function on a higher frequency and bring to an end your pain and suffering. It is our hope that all who are moving

Finding Your BLISS in the Midst of Pain

through this life would make this practice a part of their lives, so as to combat pain and suffering on a global front.

In my study and research, I have found that there are five significant times one should try to fast or should I say that it would benefit you most to fast during these times. Per Queen Afua of *Heal Thyself*, they are: (1) during your birth, which is your birth month, this is when you will be receiving many messages on how to live out the upcoming year. Remember you are the best spiritual reader of your own life. There is no one who will know you better than yourself other than the Creator. During this time, fast and pray for all doors to open spiritually and physically; (2) fast on your holy day – fast for 24 hours every week on your "holy day" or "Accra Day," which is the day the week you were born; (3) fast for every seasonal change – we do this to welcome in the new season. Fast 3, 7, or 21 days. Fasting before each season, you will prevent getting any of the illnesses that that particular season brings. You will find that fasting will assist in your body being balanced; (4) During menstruation – one should fast 2 days before the onset of your menses and then all during your menses to prevent or minimize premenstrual syndrome (PMS), headaches, pain, heavy bleeding and clotting, mood swings, and nausea. Finally, (5) fast to unblock/to clear the way – when you are experiencing blockages in your life in the form of lack or money flow, in relationships, on your job, in your profession, in your heart or health, then fast and purify to clear any lack or limitation.

In our self-care chapter we discussed the process and benefits of meditation. Here we want to mention fasting from talking, particularly during your work day, one should avoid talking for approximately 1-2 hours per day. This is merely not talking (this is when you can work on memos and send emails and such at work). This can be referred to as your 'hour of power'. We will say that this process will develop meditation opportunities. Once you peacefully close the portals called the lips, the other portals of communication become more activated, such as the "third eye" and crown chakras. From these centers you are able to "hear" the Holy Spirit talk through and to you. When you allow your chakras to open you make yourself available for the inner spiritual guidance that will come to you in your daily affairs. Another benefit of this exercise is that it helps to detoxify your thoughts and release adverse thought processes.

Dr. Camelia Straughn

CHAKRAS

NOTES

Dr. Camelia Straughn

CHAPTER 10 - Key 9

GRATITUDE

Finding Your BLISS in the Midst of Pain

So you have made it to the final chapter in this great journey of finding your *Bliss*. I am sure by now you are wondering what the finale exercise is or if there something that you will need to memorize. Please do not allow that fact that we are discussing this particular component last degrade its importance to the process of finding your *Bliss*, for it may prove to be one of the most important pieces in your journey. It is really the vehicle or practice that will keep you centered in all the other areas. Though we recognize the instrumental roles others have played in our lives, gratitude is different from indebtedness. *Gratitude*, which rhymes with "attitude," comes from the Latin word *gratus*, which means "thankful, pleasing." When you feel gratitude, you are pleased by what someone did for you and also pleased by the results. Unlike indebtedness, you're not anxious about having to pay it back. But it is still great to tell the recipient of your gratitude how much they mean to you.

Creating the habit of gratitude is something that will serve you in all areas of your life. Those who are grateful have less resentment and are usually happier people. The benefits can extend to your physical well-being, and nothing says "I love you" to your partner more than being grateful that he or she is in your life.

Thing is, people aren't hardwired to be grateful. And, like any skill worth having, gratitude requires practice. There are three stages, says Dr. Robert Emmons, author of ["Thanks! How Practicing Gratitude Can Make You Happier"](): recognizing what we're grateful for, acknowledging it, and appreciating it. Simple, right? And the benefits of practicing gratitude can be life-altering. Yet, some may find it hard to do.

- Gratitude puts situations into perspective. When we can see the good as well as the bad, it becomes more difficult to complain and stay stuck.
- Gratitude helps us realize what we have. This can lessens our need for wanting more all the time.
- Gratitude strengthens relationships, improves health, reduces stress, and, in general, makes us happier.

Here are nine ways one can cultivate gratitude:

- Notice your day-to-day world from a point of gratitude and be amazed at all the goodness we take for granted.
- Keep a gratitude journal. All it requires is noting one or more things you are

grateful for on a daily basis. No fancy notebook, no computer program required.

- If you identify something or someone with a negative trait (the cold conference room), switch it in your mind to a positive trait (the conference room with a great view).
- Gratitude requires humility, which the dictionary defines as "modest and respectful." Explore where it fits in your life. The article "Humility: A Quiet, Underappreciated Strength" is a good start.
- Give at least one compliment daily. It can be a person or it can be asking someone to share your appreciation of

something else ("I love how quiet it is in the morning, don't you?").

- When you find yourself in a bad situation ask: What can I learn? When I look back on this without emotion, what will I be grateful for?

NOTES

NOTES

Dr. Camelia Straughn

CHAPTER 11

JOURNAL

Finding Your BLISS in the Midst of Pain

Use this chapter to begin to write and reflect on the changes that you will need to make to make lasting change in your life! Remember you are always co-creating with the Universe.

Dr. Camelia Straughn

NOTES

Finding Your BLISS in the Midst of Pain
NOTES

Dr. Camelia Straughn

NOTES

NOTES

Dr. Camelia Straughn

ABOUT THE AUTHOR

Dr. Camelia Straughn is a motivational speaker, teacher, freelance writer, author, and poet. She has been the facilitator for several workshops covering women's health, sexual assault, motivational and transformational coaching, and co-parenting to name a few. She has served for over twenty years in the Army National Guard. She is the author of "Composition of a Soul's Journey through Poetry," "Women, Intimacy and Religion," and "Free Thyself: Words of Love, Pain and Victory." She currently lives in Sacramento, California with her three beautiful and amazing children and grandchildren and her lovely dog Apollo. To book or contact her go to her website at www.risingstarlifecoach.com, via email at info@risingstarlifecoach.com and risingstarlifecoach@gmail.com.

www.ingramcontent.com/pod-product-compliance
Lightning Source LLC
Chambersburg PA
CBHW041622220426
43662CB00001B/20